The Ethics
Later Pauline Letters

Colin Hart

Lecturer in Practical Theology,
St John's College Nottingham

GROVE BOOKS LIMITED
RIDLEY HALL RD CAMBRIDGE CB3 9HU

Contents

Acknowledgements

I am grateful to Rev Greg Forster and Dr Dave Leal, fellow-members of the Grove Ethics Group, for their comments on the first draft of this booklet.

The Cover Illustration is by Peter Ashton

First Impression October 2000

ISSN 1470-854X

ISBN 1 85174 446 0

1
Introduction

The main reason for describing and discussing the ethics of Colossians, Ephesians, 1 and 2 Timothy and Titus in a separate booklet from the other epistles attributed to the Apostle Paul is that they contain different kinds of ethical material and raise different questions of interpretation. In addition, most (but not all) scholars believe that these five epistles originate from a later period than those which were considered in an earlier booklet (E 115 *The Ethics of Paul*), and that some or all of them were not written by the Apostle Paul, despite bearing his name. The reason for dating these epistles late in Paul's life or after his death is that their tone, interests and attitudes seem typical of 'second-generation' Christianity, when the excitement, fervour and heroism of the first followers of Jesus have been replaced by a longer-term view, with an emphasis on stability and institutionalization. Like many arguments about the dating of biblical books, this interpretation is based on certain assumptions about the ways in which religious beliefs and institutions develop. For a summary of the arguments about authorship, see Appendix 1 .

For the sake of simplicity, I will use the phrase 'the undisputed epistles' to signify Romans, 1 & 2 Corinthians, Galatians, Philippians and 1 & 2 Thessalonians, and I will refer to Colossians, Ephesians and the Pastoral Epistles (those to Timothy and Titus) as 'the later epistles.' It is just possible that the 'later epistles' were written at about the same time as the undisputed epistles, but—if so—most of the interpretative comments of this booklet and of recent commentaries will be beside the point.

If these five epistles are all Deutero-Pauline (rather than from the hand of Paul himself), that does not mean there are no differences between them. Most scholars think that Ephesians is later than Colossians and the Pastoral Epistles are later than both of them. Macdonald (1988), examining the epistles from a sociological point of view, suggests that the undisputed epistles represent 'community-building institutionalization,' Colossians and Ephesians 'community-stabilizing institutionalization' and the Pastoral Epistles 'community-protecting institutionalization.' An alternative description is that the Pastoral Epistles represent a conservative approach to the Pauline legacy, while Colossians and Ephesians originate from what Wedderburn (in Wedderburn & Lincoln 1993, p 63) calls 'a more speculative, adventurous stream.'

One of the differences between the undisputed and the later epistles is that ethical matters feature more prominently in the latter. As I showed in the earlier booklet Paul is concerned in his undisputed epistles to convince his readers that the gospel to which they have responded involves living a moral life, and he makes practical responses to situations and questions which have arisen in the churches with which he is concerned, but he does not give systematic or detailed moral guidance for its own sake, as the authors of these later epistles do.

2
The Ethical Teaching of Colossians and Ephesians

The Imperative in the Indicative

As in the undisputed Pauline epistles, ethical exhortation in Colossians and Ephesians follows logically from theological affirmations, although some commentators judge that they lay a heavier emphasis on the ethics. The word 'therefore' or 'then' marks the turning point of both these epistles, and the connection between the indicative and the imperative, as it does in Romans 12.1. In Colossians 3.1, the Christian's experience of being 'raised with Christ' leads first to the exhortation to 'seek' and 'set your minds on' 'things above,' and secondly, in v 5 (introduced by a further 'therefore'), to the injunction to 'put to death your limbs that are on earth.' The equivalent argument in Ephesians 4.1 urges readers to 'behave worthily of the calling with which you were called,' and expounds that concept in terms of the virtues of unity.

To describe Christian conversion, both epistles use the Pauline images of resurrection (Colossians 2.13, Ephesians 2.1, 5f) and reconciliation (Colossians 1.22, Ephesians 2.13–16). The basis of the ethical arguments in Colossians 3.13 and Ephesians 4.32 is gratitude and imitation; these motifs, too, are quite consistent with the undisputed Pauline epistles, for example as at Romans 15.7.

The fundamental ethical message of these epistles is a particular form of the imperative implicit in the indicative, namely that when the readers were 'Gentiles' (Ephesians 4.17) or 'darkness' (Ephesians 5.7), evil behaviour was natural to them, but now that they have turned their backs on their pre-Christian past, and have been enlightened and renewed, such behaviour is alien to them and they should therefore eschew it. This point is related particularly to the experience of baptism. The ethical exhortation in Colossians 2.6f, for example, consists of urging readers to live consistently with the commitment they made to accept the Lordship of Christ. In Colossians 3.9–12 and its parallel, Ephesians 4.22–24, the image is of undressing and dressing, which may well have been intended as a reminder of the practice of removing clothing for baptism and putting on new clothes after being baptized. Ephesians 5.14 is probably a quotation from a baptismal hymn, which—being familiar to the readers—would have made it clear that the contrast between 'the deeds of darkness' and 'the fruit of the light' in the preceding verses refers to life before and after baptism.

Holiness in Practice

Colossians and Ephesians resemble each other with regard to practical injunctions concerning Christian behaviour, but Ephesians connects them more specifically with the concept of holiness. The theme of holiness is introduced early in Ephesians, when God's eternal purpose for his people is defined as 'that we should be holy and unblemished before him' (1.4). Holiness is also characteristic of the church as the new people of God, depicted through the image of 'a holy temple in the Lord' (2.21), while the aim of Christ's self-giving love for the church is defined in 5.26f as

> to make her holy, having cleansed her by the washing of water through the word, that he might present the church to himself glorious, not having a stain or wrinkle or anything of that kind, but that she should be holy and unblemished.

Both epistles emphasize two areas of life as places where holiness expresses itself, namely speech and sex. In Colossians 3, readers are exhorted to 'put to death' or 'put away' two groups of sins, one consisting mainly of sexual sins (v 5) and the other concerning speech (vv 8f). A few verses later, the second group is contrasted with the right use of speech, namely to edify one another and to praise God.

Two aspects of holiness in speech—truth-telling and the management of anger—are introduced in Ephesians 4.25f. These examples prepare for the main treatment of this subject, in 4.29–31, where the exhortation not to 'grieve the Holy Spirit of God' is closely connected with the use of speech. In general (v 29), speech must not be 'rotten' or 'worthless,' but should be edifying and 'give grace to those who hear.' Specifically (v 31), the sins against fellowship which readers are urged to put away are sins of speech. A few verses later, the theme of sexual holiness is introduced by a further reference to speech, in 5.3f, 12, where it seems to be suggested that talking about sexual sins—especially 'coarse joking' about them—would make them more likely to occur. The motive for abstaining from obscene talk is that such abstinence is 'proper for holy people' (5.3). In 5.19f, the right use of speech—the positive alternative to obscenity—is identified as praise.

In Ephesians 4.19, 'licentiousness,' 'all impurity' and 'greed' are identified as characteristic of 'the Gentiles.' The point of this negative description is that the author is reminding his readers of their former way of life in order (v 17) to urge them not to slip back into it. He returns to this argument in 5.5–10, assuring his readers that 'immoral, impure or greedy' persons (the same sins already identified in v 3 and almost identical with those in 4.19) do not have any 'inheritance in the kingdom of Christ and of God.'

The Unity of the Body

The unity of the church and its ethical implications are prominent themes in these two epistles. The most powerful of all the New Testament exhortations to unity occurs in Ephesians 4.1–6, where the 'call' into membership of the church is the basis, first, for a general exhortation to live 'worthily' and then in particular to an emphasis on unity, based on a list of theological themes featuring unity. The Pauline image of the church as the 'body of Christ' is developed further in vv 15f, where Christ is the 'head.' A stronger word for 'therefore' is used in v 25 to introduce a further exhortation based on shared membership of the church:

> Therefore, putting off falsehood, let each one speak truth with his neighbour, because we are members of one another.

Colossians 3.11–15 is another appeal for unity in the church. After asserting the abolition of natural human divisions (similar to Galatians 3.28), the author commends to his readers the practical virtues of unity, such as kindness, patience and forgiveness.

In fact, Sanders (1986, p 79) argues that the unity of the church is the foundation of the ethical teaching of these epistles:

> Boiled down…the ethical position of Colossians and Ephesians may be summarized as an appeal for unity in the church, which is made up of Christians who ought to make their visible, present existence like their invisible, heavenly existence and thereby show that Christians are ethically different from others.

Sanders is right to identify the theme of unity as fundamental to both these epistles. In Colossians 1.20 God's achievement in Christ is defined as 'to reconcile all things to himself,' after which the author describes the experience of reconciliation which his readers have enjoyed, thereby implicitly interpreting their experience in the context of God's eternal purpose of cosmic reconciliation. Ephesians further develops these ideas. According to Ephesians 1.9f, the aim of the epistle is to locate the work and experience of salvation in the context of the 'mystery' of God's 'plan for the fulfilment of time,' which is 'to sum up all things in Christ, things in heaven and things on earth.' The author goes straight on to explain that he and his readers coming to faith was an early stage of this work of reunification.

Love

As in Paul's undisputed epistles, the supreme virtue is love, especially as the bond which holds the fellowship together. In Colossians 3.14 the image of clothing oneself with virtues culminates in the picture of love as a girdle, which binds the other garments together. Literally, this verse says 'above all these things love, which is the bond of perfection,' and some writers—noticing that the word here translated 'bond' occurs in the plural in 2.19, where it is usually rendered 'ligaments'—have concluded that

> Taken together, 2.19 and 3.14 show that in Colossians love is presented as that which binds together the members of Christ's body just as a human body is held together by its ligaments. (Furnish 1973 p 120)

In Ephesians 3.17–19, love is the soil in which mature Christians are planted and the foundation on which they are built, while in 4.15 it qualifies the injunction to speak the truth, and in 4.16 it is identified as characteristic of authentic growth. In 4.2, however, love is given a less prominent position than in Colossians 3.14, apparently being replaced in prime position by peace. In 5.2 (preparing the way for 5.25–33) love is the appropriate response on the part of those who have experienced the love of God in Christ. Above all, the behaviour of a man towards his wife (Ephesians 5.25–33) is based on a love which is modelled on the love of Christ for the Church.

3

The Ethical Teaching of the Pastoral Epistles

The Imperative in the Indicative

The foundation of ethical exhortation and guidance in the Pastoral Epistles remains 'the indicative in the imperative,' but the emphasis on the imperative has increased still further, and the indicative is often left unstated. Schrage (1988, p 257) goes so far as to claim that in these epistles,

> For the most part parenesis stands unrelated to the indicative. Its content is more traditional, set down didactically in fixed rules of conduct and morality.

The indicative is certainly not absent from the Pastoral Epistles, however. Titus 3.4–7, for example, brings together many of Paul's own favourite motifs, mostly expressed in his vocabulary, although viewed from the perspective of the individual subjective experience of salvation rather than the objective, once for all work of Christ. Indicative and imperative are explicitly linked in Titus 2.11–14, which is also quite Pauline in thought. The motivation for holy living in this passage is both a response to the saving work of God (vv 11 and 14) and a preparation for the 'appearing' (epiphany) of Christ (v 13).

Bourgeois Morality?

Since Martin Dibelius summed up the ethical stance of the Pastoral Epistles in the phrase *christliche Bürgerlichkeit* (translated as 'good Christian citizenship' in the English version of the 4th edition of his commentary, Dibelius and Conzelmann 1972), many commentators have agreed with him that these epistles inculcate a bourgeois morality. In Conzelmann's edition of the commentary, these comments are toned down, but not denied. Dibelius and Conzelmann themselves (p 39) define the difference between the attitude of the author of the Pastorals and Paul himself (or the early Paul):

> Paul lives in the tension between this world and God's world. He joyfully affirmed (in 2 Cor 6.4–10) the suffering of this existence as part of citizenship in the other kingdom. The author of the Pastorals seeks to build the possibility of a life in this world, although on the basis of Christian principles. He wishes to become part of the world. Thus, for him, the peace of a secure life is a goal of the Christian.

Kidd 1990 has helpfully identified three aspects of 'good Christian citizenship,' which seem to be implied by Dibelius's use of the term, namely that the church of the Pastorals is 'socially ascendant,' 'culturally accommodative' and 'unheroically conservative.'

An important strand of Dibelius's argument concerned the interpretation of the word *eusebeia*, which recent translations of the New Testament generally render as 'godliness,' and which is the central virtue in the Pastoral Epistles. Dibelius and his followers emphasize the fact that *eusebeia* is the Greek equivalent for the Latin *pietas*, and interpret it as meaning respectfulness and respectability, although Dibelius and Conzelmann (1972, p 39) offer a more balanced interpretation:

> As seldom as this term occurs elsewhere in the Greek Bible, so frequently it appears in the inscriptions. It designates not only the fulfilment of special cultic duties but also the general behaviour which is pleasing to God.

More recent writers, especially Towner 1989, have shown that in Hellenistic Judaism *eusebeia* and its cognates signified 'the fear of the Lord,' a concept which combined a relationship with God and a quality of behaviour, and they think that is the background of the usage in these epistles.

The first occurrence of the word, in 1 Timothy 2.2, supports Dibelius's interpretation, for here *eusebeia* is closely connected with political loyalty and good citizenship, and the goal is 'that we may live a peaceful and tranquil life in all *eusebeia* and dignity.' Not only *eusebeia* but also the last word in this clause (*semnotes*) has a range of meanings, which is why the Revised Standard Version can render the last phrase as 'godly and respectful in every way,' while the New International Version subverts Dibelius's criticism in its translation 'in all godliness and holiness.'

Although this verse does support Dibelius's interpretation of *eusebeia*, it is the only place where such connotations are explicit. On the basis of all the occurrences of the word, Marshall (1999, p 144) concludes that

> as employed in the Pastoral Epistles, *eusebeia* expresses a strongly Christian concept of the new existence in Christ that combines belief in God and a consequent manner of life.

Other qualities commended in the Pastoral Epistles are 'self-control,' 'discipline' and 'sobriety.' The triad 'sober, upright and godly' (referring to three of the four Greek 'cardinal virtues') is stated in Titus 2.12 as a summary of the qualities which should characterize the lives of Christians. Despite the frequent allegation that the Pastoral Epistles encourage their readers to accommodate themselves to the standards of the world, the first half of that verse exhorts them to 'renounce ungodliness and worldly desires.'

Some of the ethical teaching in the Pastorals is amongst the evidence cited by those who believe they could not have been written by the author of the major epistles. Three times in 1 Timothy (1.5, 1.19 and 3.9) and once in 2 Timothy (1.3), the writer speaks of himself or his readers as having a 'good' or 'pure' conscience. *Dikaiosyne* in 1 Timothy 6.11, 2 Timothy 2.22 and 2 Timothy 3.16 is clearly an ethical quality, and rightly translated as 'righteousness,' while the cognate verb in Titus 3.7 is rightly rendered as 'justified.' I showed in the earlier booklet, however, that this ambiguity between the forensic and ethical senses of these words is characteristic of Paul's undisputed epistles. The attitude to the Old Testament Law expressed in 1 Timothy 1.8—'We know that the Law is good, if anyone uses it lawfully'—is often alleged to be spectacularly unPauline, but it is, in fact, quite similar to the attitude towards the Law displayed by Paul himself in Romans 7.12–16.

Moral Qualifications for Leadership

Three passages in the Pastoral Epistles describe the qualifications for church leaders. 1 Timothy 3.1–7 and Titus 1.6–9 deal with 'bishops,' or overseers, and 1 Timothy 3.8–13 with deacons.

The fundamental requirement for 'bishops' in 1 Timothy 3 is to be 'irreproachable' and in Titus 1 to be 'blameless.' 1 Timothy 3.7 emphasizes the concern for reputation (literally 'testimony') among outsiders. Both passages expand these general requirements by means of similar lists, although the vocabulary is mostly different. Some of the qualities required are general (such as to be self-controlled, respectable and sober), while others relate specifically to leadership style (such as 'not arrogant, not quick-tempered…not seeking dishonest gain'), and still others refer to the gifts required for the work of church leadership (such as hospitality and teaching ability). There is an explicit connection, especially in 1 Timothy 3.5, between the qualities and guidelines required for household management and those appropriate for leadership in the church. According to both passages, only those who manage their own households successfully are fit to manage the household of God. So a bishop's children must be submissive and respectful (1 Timothy), not profligate or rebellious (Titus). Titus probably also requires the children to be believers, although Towner argues for the translation 'trustworthy.' Both lists include 'the husband of one wife,' a phrase which suggests a contrast with some other state—but there are good reasons why this other state is unlikely to be celibacy, polygamy or remarriage after widowhood or divorce. So most recent commentators, including Towner and Marshall, think the phrase probably refers to faithfulness in marriage.

The deacon code closely resembles the two bishop codes. The basic requirement to be 'blameless' is expounded in very similar terms to the other two lists. The only significant difference is that the 'women'—who may be female deacons or deacons' wives—are also required to be 'serious, not slanderers, temperate, faithful in all things.'

Some writers have pointed out that the historical Paul himself might not have qualified as a bishop or deacon by these criteria, but Brown (1984, p 35) has rightly responded,

> Rough vitality and a willingness to fight bare-knuckled for the gospel were part of what made Paul a great missionary, but such characteristics might have made him a poor residential community supervisor. The Pastorals are listing qualities necessary for someone who would have to get along with a community for a long time; fortunately for all, perhaps, Paul's missionary genius kept him on the move.

Moderation

It is characteristic of the Pastoral Epistles to recommend moderation as a virtue. In particular, the reader is encouraged to enjoy food and moderate amounts of wine, while avoiding drunkenness; the reader should flee youthful desires, but young women are encouraged to marry; and although the dangers of riches are emphasized, it seems to be taken for granted that members of the church will own some property.

In 1 Timothy 6.6–8, the ideals at which to aim are moderation and *autarkeia*, translated as 'self-sufficiency' or 'contentment.' This attitude is contrasted with that of the false teachers. Whereas they imagine that *eusebeia* is a means of 'gain,' there is actually great 'gain' in *eusebeia* plus *autarkeia*. This latter virtue was much commended by Greek moral teachers, and Paul uses it in Philippians 4.11 to describe his own attitude.

Schrage (1988, p 262) draws attention to the condemnation of drunkenness in 1 Timothy 3.3, 8, and Titus 1.7, 2.3, and interprets 1 Timothy 5.23 as recommending moderate use of wine:

> In other words, neither no wine nor much wine, but some wine. This middle road between total abstinence and drunkenness well characterizes the attitude of the Pastorals to worldly goods and pleasures.

Other commentators, however, have emphasized the specifically limited context of the favourable evaluation of wine: Marshall (1999, p 624), for example, protests

> Even to say that the moderate use of alcohol is *recommended* goes rather beyond the *permission* to use it for health reasons. Nothing is said that criticizes Timothy's fundamental attitude. The claim that the recommendation is part of the 'bourgeois' ethic of the author which is concerned with what is practicable and withdraws from any kind of heroic asceticism completely misses the point.

Church leaders and other Christians are expected to have a right attitude towards money. In 1 Timothy 6.5, 2 Timothy 3.2 and Titus 1.11, greed for money is one of the accusations levelled against the false teachers, although this may be a conventional insult rather than a serious allegation. Conversely, 1 Timothy 3.3, 8 and Titus 1.7 instruct bishops and deacons not to be 'greedy for gain.'

1 Timothy 6.9f is aimed at 'those who want to be rich,' while vv 17–19 are directed towards those who are already 'rich in the present age.' Macdonald (1988, p 201) summarizes the attitudes of this chapter as

> A condemnation of the accumulation of wealth, coupled with an acceptance of already established wealth on the condition that the wealthy recognize their responsibility to the poor.

Many commentators draw a contrast between 1 Timothy 6.17–19 and the attitude of Jesus himself or the gospels towards wealth. The gospels are, however, not as univocal on this matter as some writers imagine. As I showed in an earlier booklet in this series (E 111, *The Ethics of the Gospels*) Luke, at least, does not regard rich Christians as a contradiction in terms, but offers them some support and guidance in their attempts to live out their religious commitment.

Charity in Action

The story in Acts 6 concerning complaints and jealousy over the church's charitable work amongst the widows within its membership is well known. 1 Timothy 5.3–16 discusses from a practical point of view certain other questions arising from a similar situation in a different location.

The author carefully differentiates between three categories of widows: those who have relatives who can and therefore must care for them; those who are young enough to remarry and play a full part in the community; and 'real widows.' According to vv 6 and 9, part of the definition of a 'real widow' is that she should not be self-indulgent but with a reputation for good deeds. Schrage contrasts this careful, pragmatic and rather moralistic approach to charitable action with the gospels, asking

> whether the Good Samaritan could have interrogated the traveller who fell among thieves about the morality of his life before offering help

but he admits that questions of this kind did need to be asked, since the resources available for charitable work were severely limited, and fair, practicable solutions did need to be devised and implemented.

Love

Like the other books in the New Testament, the Pastoral Epistles identify love as a significant virtue, but it is not as pre-eminent here as in the undisputed epistles or even in Colossians and Ephesians. Its relationship to other virtues is expressed in 1 Timothy 6.11, where the reader is urged to 'pursue righteousness, *eusebeia*, faith, love, endurance, gentleness.' In nine of the ten occurrences of the word in the Pastoral Epistles, love is closely associated with faith (but not with hope, the third member of the triad in 1 Corinthians 13.13 and elsewhere); Towner (1989 p 162) points out that because faith represents the 'vertical dimension of Christian existence' while love expresses the 'horizontal dimension,' it is not surprising to find them closely linked. By contrast wth the false teachers, according to 1 Timothy 1.5, the goal of the command is love out of a pure heart and of a good conscience and of sincere faith, while in Titus 2.2 love is one of the qualities which should be exhibited by older men.

4
Asceticism

Like most of the New Testament, these five epistles are partly or wholly polemical documents. Many of the emphases—such as the portrayal of the church as institution and the responsibilities of bishops and deacons in the Pastoral Epistles—may well be aspects of the authors' response to the danger of false teaching. One strand of the dispute seems to have been asceticism, which is explicitly discussed in Colossians and 1 Timothy.

The identification of the opponents whose activities lie behind these epistles is a complex and ambiguous process. The epistles themselves may be unreliable witnesses, because their authors aim to criticize the people they regard as false teachers and to deter people from following them, not to expound their views fairly. Some later witnesses give more information about their own opponents—such as quoting from their writings—but it is unclear how far those trends had developed in New Testament times. The false teachers being attacked in Colossians and 1 Timothy may represent tendencies which in more developed forms subsequently became known as Gnostic, but it would be anachronistic to apply that adjective to those teachers themselves. Dualism between the spiritual and the physical led adherents of these movements to differentiate between the Supreme and Holy God and an inferior creator. This low view of creation sometimes encouraged ascetic practices, whereby people attempted to free the soul from the trammels of the body by denying bodily appetites, especially food and sex.

In Colossians 2.16, 20–23 the author warns his readers against a collection of false teachings, which may or may not have constituted a single coherent theological position and may have originated from a Gentile or a Jewish source. Recent commentators, including Dunn (1996), have tended to interpret these references in terms of the practices of Judaism; if this is correct, then the argument is very similar to the attitude of the author of the undisputed epistles, even though the vocabulary may be different. Whatever the ideological background may have been, the teachers whom this epistle criticizes were evidently discouraging the satisfaction of certain physical needs or pleasures, as a way of growing in holiness. The heart of this author's response is v 23, in which he explains that practices which treat the *body* (*soma*) harshly do not help to check the indulgence of the *flesh* (*sarx*)—which the New International Version of the Bible renders in most occurrences as 'the sinful nature' but here as 'sensual indulgence.'

Similarly, 1 Timothy 4.3 states that the false teachers forbid marriage and certain foods. In reply (v 4), the author presents a positive doctrine of creation, from which he deduces that 'nothing which is received with thanksgiving should be rejected.' The encouragement for young widows to remarry (1 Timothy 5.14) and the commendation of childbirth (1 Timothy 2.15) may also be responses to a movement which deprecated marriage and sex.

5
Household Codes

Colossians 3.18–4.1 and Ephesians 5.22–6.9 consist of teaching on relationships within the household, presented as three pairs of injunctions, addressed to wives and husbands, children and parents, and slaves and masters. The children were not necessarily below the age of adulthood. The Ephesian household code appears to be a heavily edited version of the one in Colossians. Whereas Colossians lays more emphasis on the slave/master relationship, Ephesians greatly expands the teaching on relations between husbands and wives.

Similar material, but with the emphasis on the duties of the subordinate member of the pair, occurs in the Pastoral Epistles, particularly 1 Timothy 2.9–15 and Titus 2.4f on the duties of wives and 1 Timothy 6.1f and Titus 2.9f on the duties of slaves, and in 1 Peter 2.18–3.7 (slaves, wives and husbands). Titus 2.1–10 is, in fact, as systematic and structured as the Colossian and Ephesian household codes, dealing in order with the duties of old men, old women, young women, young men and slaves. It is widely believed that all these passages, together with similar material in some of the Fathers, are variations of a single basic pattern of ethical teaching. Following Luther, the German word *haustafel* is often used to denote these household codes.

The household codes in Colossians and Ephesians assume that all parties in the household relationships are Christians, whereas the equivalent passage in 1 Peter concentrates on advising Christians how to behave when the other party is not a Christian. Best (1998, p 524) identifies more than a dozen questions which must frequently have arisen, but on which the household code in Ephesians offers no guidance. The version in 1 Peter also focuses more widely than the household, for 2.13–17 deal with relations with political authorities.

1 Timothy 2.11–15 also attributes a subordinate position to women, but in this case in the context of the church, where women are forbidden to teach or exercise authority over men.

The scholarly consensus for several decades followed Dibelius in interpreting the New Testament household codes as lightly Christianized versions of a non-Christian code, which the church took from its original Stoic sources either directly or by way of Hellenistic Judaism. Crouch (1972) and Balch (1988) have, however, shown that Dibelius and his followers overstated the similarity between the Hellenistic and Christian material.

Recent scholars have emphasized the influence of Aristotle's discussion of 'household management.' In ancient times, the household was the foundation of the state and of religion, and interest in household relationships was so widespread in the cultural background against which the New Testament was written that it was only to be expected that Christian writers would discuss them, and it is futile to attempt to identify any particular pagan writer or school as the direct source of the Christian material.

The current scholarly consensus is that there is no precise analogy to the form and theme of the New Testament household codes, although many Greek and Jewish sources discuss the theme of household relationships and a few even resemble the New Testament material in viewing the relationships from both sides. The subject-matter and ethos of the codes in Colossians and Ephesians do embody typical first-century assumptions, but if they were derived from a particular Hellenistic-Jewish or popular philosophical source it has not survived.

Since household management was regarded as so important, one possible motive for the Christian discussions of the subject may have been a desire to reassure their neighbours that they were politically conservative and did not present a threat to the stability of society. Barth (1974 p 661) draws a parallel with 1 Corinthians 11.5–10 and 14.33–35, and suggests that both women and slaves in Ephesus may have been asserting their freedom in ways which the author of Ephesians considered inappropriate. Best (1998, p 524) rightly retorts that the absence of any reference to the outside world in the Ephesian household code (unlike that in 1 Peter) counts against the theory that its motivation is apologetic or evangelistic, but in Titus 2.5 the motivation for wives to submit to their husbands is explicitly 'lest the word of God be insulted.'

The theological basis of both household codes is the Lordship of Christ, but this theology is more thoroughly developed and integrated in Ephesians. The submission of wives is described in Colossians as 'fitting in the Lord' and the obedience of children as 'pleasing to [literally 'in'] the Lord,' but the corresponding injunctions to husbands and fathers are not given an explicit theological basis. The main distinctive feature of the Ephesian code is an extended comparison between the relationship of husband and wife and that of Christ and the church. The duty of children to obey their parents according to Ephesians is 'right' and is also one of the Ten Commandments. The exhortations to slaves in Colossians are based on a fourfold grounding in the Lordship of Christ ('fearing the Lord,' 'as to the Lord,' reward from the Lord and 'serving the Lord'), and the duty of slave-owners to treat their slaves fairly is based on the fact that they, too, have a 'master'; the equivalent sections in Ephesians are very similar.

6
Ethical Criticisms of the Later Pauline Epistles

Three main criticisms of the later Pauline epistles have been made by recent commentators. The first concerns the ethics of pseudonymity; the second criticizes these writings for being less heroic and more given to compromise than the gospels and Paul's undisputed epistles; and the third criticizes the conservatism of the epistles from a modern perspective, claiming that they endorse unjust relationships.

Pseudonymity

There are four ways of evaluating the ethical teaching of these epistles in the light of the questions which have been raised concerning the identity of their author. The most obvious approach is to assert that the teaching carries Paul's own apostolic authority, because he wrote it. However, the cumulative evidence against attributing the epistles to Paul himself is so strong that to base the authority of the teaching on authorship is distinctly precarious.

The second approach is the opposite of the first, arguing that since the ethical teaching is explicitly based on Paul's own apostolic authority, and there are good reasons for suspecting that he did not write the epistles, the teaching should be rejected. Recent commentators have, however, pointed out the dangers inherent in this approach, whereby the prejudices of the modern reader are used as the basis for constructing a 'canon within the canon.'

Thirdly, some commentators focus on canonicity, claiming that whoever wrote these epistles, they carry authority for Christian readers because—recognizing them as inspired—the church has included them in the canon of the New Testament. Since, however one of the main reasons for including these epistles in the canon was because Paul was believed to have written them, this approach fails to resolve the problem.

Fourthly, it may be possible to take a more moderate approach, neither to attribute nor to deny authority to this ethical teaching by reference to extrinsic factors, but to evaluate the contents by asking the questions posed by Young (1992, p 120):

> To what extent is the claim of these texts that they pass on the authoritative tradition of Paul valid? In what ways is that tradition appropriately developed further for a new situation?

This is also the approach taken by Dunn (1996) to Colossians. He claims (p 39) that since the teaching of that epistle is so recognizably an authentic development of the thought of Paul's undisputed epistles, it really does not matter whether it was written by Paul himself, later in life, or by one of his associates, writing either under Paul's instructions or after his death.

Compromise

Sanders (1986) criticizes Colossians, Ephesians and especially the Pastoral Epistles by comparison with the undisputed epistles for being insufficiently distinctive from their surroundings. According to him, and several writers of the previous generation, authentic Christian ethics should be heroic, and stand in judgment on the values and behaviour of their age, but instead the later Pauline epistles appear to endorse those values and encourage Christians to live just like their neighbours. Accepting Dibelius's claim that the NT household codes were taken over, almost unchanged, from pagan sources, Sanders describes them (p 75) as

> completely worthless for Christian ethics. Coming early into the post-Pauline tradition, they do not even serve a useful function for the authors of Colossians and Ephesians; for the *Haustafeln* cannot truly be guides (in spite of the attempt in Col 3.22) for helping to bring this life into harmony with the life beyond unless the life beyond is really no different from the non-Christian world—something that both authors would hotly deny. The *Haustafeln*, by the same token, do not mark off Christian existence from non-Christian existence, since the regulations are by and large derived from non-Christian sources.

This criticism has generally been a Protestant phenomenon, and has been linked with the identification of 'early Catholicism' in these writings, an approach which regards the institutionalization of the church as marking the end of its authenticity. Most recent writers who articulate this evaluation, however, do so in order to disagree with it, arguing that these epistles fulfilled a necessary task, giving to the church realistic guidelines for Christian living in the absence of a sense of eschatological urgency. Dunn (1996, p 245) comments that Sanders

> quite fails to see that believers were being urged *not* to be different at this point, but to live fully in accord with high social ideals, widely esteemed as such by other ethicists of the time. The perspective and enabling might be different, but the goals were shared. That others share their high standards of social behaviour and *vice versa* should never be an embarrassment to Christians.

This more positive evaluation of the ethical teaching of Colossians, Ephesians and the Pastoral Epistles has in recent decades developed into a consensus. Furthermore, if these epistles were intended to persuade outsiders that the church was politically innocuous, 1 Timothy 2.2–4 implies that the underlying motive was mission rather than a desire for a quiet and safe life.

Even if there are obvious similarities between the ethical teaching of these epistles and certain non-Christian writers, it does not follow that the epistles minimize the differences between the behaviour which they regard as *typical* of the world and of the church. On the contrary, as Matera (1996, p 220) expresses it,

> Paul draws a sharp contrast between these two kinds of existence, suggesting that there is no good in the world and no wrong in the church.

One aspect of this issue concerns the qualities identified by the Pastoral Epistles as required of church leaders. The contemporary church is sometimes criticized for the criteria it applies in selecting its ministers. Critics (including preachers and students writing assignments in Practical Theology) who seek guidance on the form and style of the church from the New Testament usually turn first to the gospels and the undisputed epistles of Paul, and point out, for example, that the apostles whom Jesus chose might not have been 'recommended for training' if they had attended a Selection Conference for ordained ministry. But this is to overlook both the differences which two thousand years of history may have made, and the major differences between the ministry of Jesus and Paul and the needs of a settled church. It would be wise for anyone seeking guidance from the New Testament on this issue to overcome his or her prejudice against 'early Catholicism' and look to the later Pauline letters, for those documents are trying to answer similar questions to our own. Brown (1984, p 34) comments

> Jesus during his ministry called prominent followers from various walks of life without any consideration how society might look on fishermen, tax collectors and a zealot. But Jesus was not structuring a society; he did not live in an organized church; the Twelve were selected not as administrators but as eschatological judges of the renewed Israel. Once the movement associated with Christ became organized enough to be a society called 'church,' however, it began to decide that certain standards of religious respectability were very important for the common good. Individuals, however talented, who did not meet those standards would have to be sacrificed.

Brown goes on, however, to point out (p 41) that dangers as well as benefits are implicit in this argument, and in the approach of the Pastoral Epistles to the qualities required for church leadership:

> The 'clergy' appointed by Timothy and Titus should have been good, sound people, easy to get along with as resident pastors, but their job profile is not likely to have brought to leadership dynamic 'movers' who would change the world.

There is a connection between this objection to the ethics of the later Pauline Epistles and the next objection to be considered. However worthy the motives which led the writers to encourage their readers to follow the social and domestic conventions of their day, the use of this material and the development of these ideas in subsequent generations protected those conventions from being subjected to proper ethical and theological scrutiny, with the result that inequality between the sexes and between social classes was accepted for too long. As Wedderburn (1993, p 57) comments,

> an endorsement of the *status quo* would only be avoided if bringing these conventions under the authority of the Lord brought about a radical reappraisal of them, a questioning whether these relationships reflected the character of the Lord. There is little sign in Colossians of that happening…

Inequality

Much of this ethical teaching—especially the household codes—poses a difficult hermeneutical problem for readers in the early twenty-first century, because it apparently endorses a hierarchical ordering of family and work relationships which nowadays many people (at least in Americo-European culture) would heartily reject. Young (1994, p 146) is a particularly clear example of this criticism. Although her comments refer explicitly to the Pastoral Epistles, the same principles could be applied to Colossians and Ephesians, especially the household codes. Extrapolating from a feminist reading, Young argues that the worldview of these epistles 'reinforces patriarchal hierarchy in family, society and church,' thereby confronting modern views of the position of women, servants and lay-people. She claims (p 147) that the theology of the Pastoral Epistles

> presents us with a whole culture of subordination. The Roman imperial system has been sacralized. No matter how kindly the Supreme Ruler be presented, an inherently oppressive social order has been projected onto the heavens. The problems of this picture are compounded by a view of 'teaching' which we might well characterize as oppressively dogmatic and authoritative, an educative process integrated into this monarchical authority-structure, with no sense of training a person to be free and independent, creative, or autonomous in taking responsibility for his or her own actions.

Commentators have responded to this problem in four ways.

1. Literal Interpretation

The approach which takes these passages literally, and regards role differences between men and women or at least husbands and wives as God-given, is much less widespread than it was a few decades ago. Among recent commentators, O'Brien (1999, p 408) favours a literal interpretation of the household code in Ephesians. After emphasizing that 'the value, dignity or worth of the members of the Christian household in a subordinate position is no less than that of those in authority,' he concludes:

> Theologically, we are not free to retain a supposedly exalted view of Christian marriage with its loving service, commitment, trust and growth, on the one hand, and to jettison hierarchical patterns of submission, or subordination, on the other, because they are expressions of an outmoded first-century worldview that are unacceptable in our contemporary situation.

Most preachers and writers who interpret the household codes in this way place considerable emphasis on their ideological foundation. Whereas Hellenistic teaching on household relationships is derived from reason or natural law, these documents ground their exhortations in Christian theology, particularly being 'in' or 'to the Lord,' which arguably both makes them more binding and transforms the way they happen in practice. But Wedderburn (1993, p 56) pointedly asks,

> is all this any more than lending a Christian endorsement to the thoroughly patriarchal norms of society of the day?

Although the literal interpretation has the merit of simplicity, it is deeply offensive to many people both inside and outside the church. That offensiveness is, of course, not necessarily sufficient reason to reject the interpretation, since Christians generally expect to judge their own lives by the standards of Scripture, not *vice versa*.

2. Revisionist Interpretation

Some commentators have sought to avoid this criticism of these epistles by claiming that the more offensive elements of their ethical teaching do not mean what previous generations of translators and readers imagined they meant. In particular, it has been suggested that the grammar of the word usually translated as 'submit' or 'be subject' in Colossians 3.18, Ephesians 5.21–24 and Titus 2.5, 9 implies that the inequality is voluntary—but conceding this point does little to mitigate the offensiveness of the passage. Although the word 'submit' does not actually occur in the second half of Ephesians 5.24 and probably not in v 22, the logic of both passages requires it to be understood. It is possible that the description of a husband as the 'head' of the wife in Ephesians 5.23 refers to origin more than to authority, but even if this is so, the concept is still being used as the basis for urging wives to be submissive towards their husbands. Similarly, many attempts have been made to evade the prohibition expressed in 1 Timothy 2.11f against women teaching or having authority over men in church.

3. Emphasis on Distinctives

The approach to this material which is probably most widely held among recent commentators is to emphasize those aspects which are most congenial to modern thinking, identifying them as distinctively Christian, and to explain away the offensive features as merely part of the cultural background. Dibelius's claim that the household codes in the New Testament are revisions of a Stoic original is sometimes used as the basis for concentrating attention on the elements which were allegedly introduced by the Christian editor. Since, however, the relationship between Christian and pagan material is now known to have been much less close and direct than Dibelius realized, then the confident identification of the distinctively Christian additions is more problematic.

Commentators who approach the household codes in this way often concentrate on the version in Ephesians, since the allegedly distinctive Christian features are most prominent there. In particular, it is argued that two features of the Ephesian code deconstruct the apparent inequality of these exhortations by introducing the concept of mutuality.

Firstly, many interpreters have claimed that the whole household code in Ephesians follows logically from the preceding verse, 5.21, and should be understood in the light of the principle of mutual submission. However, the remainder of the code appears to apply the principle of submission to the subordinate member of each pair only, and not to both parties. Furthermore, the equivalent passage in Colossians is not qualified by the same over-arching principle.

Secondly, many commentators have found it significant that these codes address both parties in the relationship, whereas the Hellenistic equivalents generally concentrate on instructing the superior party in his duties to those under his authority. It is, however, not obvious why an increased emphasis on the duty of the inferior party in the relationship to submit to the authority of the superior should be regarded as particularly enlightened. Although both sides of each relationship are recognized, no rights are attributed to the subordinate party. Some commentators have suggested that it is a virtue of the codes to recognize wives, children and slaves as responsible moral agents, to whom ethical exhortation and guidance may appropriately be addressed, but Schrage (1988, pp 265–7) significantly uses the opposite argument in his discussion of the equivalent passages in the Pastoral Epistles, regarding them as inferior to the household codes themselves precisely because they put all the moral responsibility onto the subordinate party and do not balance those injunctions with any instructions as to how to exercise authority.

Opinions vary as to how thoroughly household relationships are redefined by these emphases in the household codes. Hays (1996, p 65) discerns in the codes the seeds of more enlightened ideas:

> When masters are told to stop threatening their slaves because 'you have the same Master in heaven, and with him there is no partiality' (6.9), a theological image is invoked that unsettles the conventional patterns of master-slave relations. Similarly, if marriage is a metaphor for the relationship between Christ and the church, the exalted ecclesiology of Ephesians must deconstruct static, patriarchal notions of marriage.

Lincoln (1990, p 392), by contrast, while acknowledging that marital relations in the Ephesian code are transformed by being made dependent on the over-arching exhortation to 'submit to one another in the fear of Christ' and on Christ as the model for the exercise of the husband's headship, nevertheless warns that those important insights should not be overstated, because husbands and wives in the code are still unequal, and the point of view of the argument remains irredeemably androcentric.

4. Radical Appropriation

In addition to emphasizing the offensive elements which cannot be removed from the portrayal of marital relationships in the Ephesian household code, Lincoln also draws attention to the limitations of this rather idealized portrayal of marriage as a guide for Christians seeking to engage with the issues which actually occur in real marriages. His own preferred approach is

> to see this vision of marriage for what it is—conditioned by the cultural assumptions of its time—and to appreciate what it attempts to accomplish in its

> own setting—bringing its interpretation of the Pauline gospel to bear on the household structures of its society to produce a distinctive adaptation of those structures. Contemporary Christians can best appropriate it by realizing that they are to attempt to do something similar in their own setting—to bring to bear what they hold to be the heart of the Christian message on the marriage conventions of their time.

On this basis, Lincoln suggests that a modern Christian should emphasize equality between husbands and wives, but he does not admit quite how ironic is his claim that the way to appropriate the household codes today is to teach the opposite of what they actually say.

Young (1994) takes a similar approach to the Pastoral Epistles. She regards the reader and the text as 'the two parties to a kind of conversation...in which the aim is to do justice to both sides' (p 149), and suggests (p 151) that

> it is precisely as they grapple with specific challenges...that the Pastorals point the way for others who would be true to their tradition as they grapple with new and different challenges now.

Young identifies several qualities and principles which modern readers can derive from the Pastoral Epistles, and argues (p 153):

> To be true to this perspective requires not the reproduction of the Pastorals' particular ethical maxims so much as a parallel movement to embrace what is universally true and good in the particular social and cultural context in which we find ourselves, while reserving the right to be critical, to jettison value-systems that undermine the moral qualities that are common to decent human life and the gospel.

7
Conclusion

A difficulty implicit in the task of writing earlier in this series (on Jesus, the gospels and Paul) was that readers of the New Testament have tended to be more interested in ethics than the writers were. In these later Pauline epistles, by contrast, ethics plays a major part.

Despite the serious questions which have been raised about the identity of their author, widespread agreement has developed among scholars that Colossians, Ephesians and the Pastoral Epistles are authentically Pauline in a much deeper sense than merely that they bear his name, but there is no consensus as to precisely what that deeper sense is. All of these epistles apply the fundamental principles and implications of the Apostle Paul's theology to the setting of churches which seek to survive long-term, to be accepted by the wider community and to persuade some of their neighbours to join them.

As far as ethics is concerned, these epistles achieve two main things. First, they endorse and develop the Apostle Paul's assertion that there is an essential connection between the experience of salvation and living a holy life. Secondly, they give more guidance than the undisputed epistles do on how that holy life works out in practice in concrete situations and relationships, urging their readers to earn the respect of their neighbours by the quality of their lives.

The outstanding problem is the endorsement by these epistles of unequal, hierarchical relationships in the home and at work. If a literal interpretation of those exhortations contravenes major theological themes which are perceived as fundamental to the gospel and to the Christian worldview, then readers are justified in declining to interpret them literally, although the existence of those passages within the canon of the New Testament should at least challenge readers to ensure that what they believe to be fundamental Christian principles really are so, and have not been adopted unconsciously and uncritically from the surrounding culture. Probably the least unsatisfactory approach is a combination of the third and fourth of the interpretative methods I identified above—that is, to concentrate on the distinctive insights which these writers contributed to the consideration of these subjects, and on the principles which motivated them to take the positions they did, and to apply those insights and principles creatively to the circumstances and issues of our own day.

The task of Christian ethics is not a simple one. It is not possible to discover in the later Pauline epistles—or anywhere else in the Bible—clear and unambiguous answers to complex moral questions. But reflection on relevant biblical material is an essential element of the work of Christian ethics, and Colossians, Ephesians and the Pastoral Epistles have vitally important insights to offer in that respect.

Appendix 1
Later Paul or Deutero-Paul?

The reasons for doubting that these epistles were written by Paul himself are linguistic, literary and theological.

The *linguistic* arguments are based on vocabulary and style. Several writers have made use of computers to confirm that the later epistles were not written by the same person as the undisputed epistles, but there is so much variation among the results as to cast doubt on the method. The words of Dunn (1996, p 35) concerning Colossians express the linguistic evidence against Pauline authorship of all these epistles:

> The fact is that at point after point in the letter the commentator is confronted with features characteristic of flow of thought and rhetorical technique that are consistently and markedly different from those of the undisputed Paulines...The difference comes at the authorial level—the 'fingerprint' differences of (unconscious) speech mannerisms and (second nature) patterns of composition.

The *literary* arguments for doubting that Paul himself wrote these epistles are based on the point of view of the implied author and on the difference between the stated recipients of the epistles and the implied reader. Both the portrayal of Paul and the presentation of the issues considered in these epistles appear to have been written from a later perspective than the Apostle's own lifetime.

The *theological* reasons for denying that Paul himself wrote these epistles are that some major themes of the undisputed epistles (such as justification, the union of the believer with Christ, the power of the Holy Spirit and freedom from the Law) are less prominent in Colossians, Ephesians or the Pastorals, whereas various themes which are emphasized in the latter are absent from the undisputed epistles, and that the understanding of major doctrines which are common to all these traditions—such as Christology and ecclesiology—is more developed in the later epistles. Some recent commentators, however, such as Marshall (1999), have pointed out that the similarities of doctrine are actually more striking than the differences, which generally consist of vocabulary or emphasis rather than content.

A further important factor in the discussion of the authorship of these Epistles is the phenomenon of pseudepigraphy in the 1st century. If it could be shown that it was common practice to write in the name of an illustrious predecessor as a gesture of homage or as a way of claiming to record or reapply the master's teaching, especially if this practice did not, and was not intended to, deceive the readers, then it would not be difficult to imagine that Colossians, Ephesians and the Pastoral Epistles were examples of this practice. There are certainly cases in Jewish, classical and Christian culture of documents being rejected as forgeries, and also of writings being accepted as genuine which modern scholars now think were actually pseudonymous, but it is doubtful if documents were ever accepted as authoritative even though it was known that the named authors did not really write them. On the basis of an exhaustive study of the subject, Donelson (1986, p 11) concludes:

> No one ever seems to have accepted a document as religiously and philosophically prescriptive which was known to be forged. I do not know a single example.

Conservative commentators tend to argue that these epistles should be attributed to Paul himself unless there is overwhelming evidence to the contrary and—since the evidence is less than overwhelming—they conclude that Paul wrote them. Those commentators, on the contrary, who regard the authorship of these epistles as an open question generally go with the weight of the evidence and judge that someone else wrote them in Paul's name. An intermediate view held by some scholars, including (tentatively) Hays (1996), is that Paul himself wrote Colossians, but Ephesians and the Pastorals are pseudonymous.

Appendix 2
References and Recommended Reading

Balch, David L, 1988, 'Household Codes' in David E Aune (ed), *Greco-Roman Literature and the New Testament: Selected Forms and Genres* (Atlanta: Scholars Press).

Barth, M, 1974, *Ephesians 4–6* (Anchor Bible, New York: Doubleday).

Barth, M and H Blanke, 1994, *Colossians* (Anchor Bible, New York: Doubleday).

Best, Ernest, 1998, *Ephesians* (ICC, Edinburgh: T & T Clark).

Brown, Raymond E, SS, 1984, *The Churches the Apostles Left Behind* (London: Geoffrey Chapman).

Crouch, J E, 1972, *The Origin and Intention of the Colossian Haustafel* (Gottingen: Vandenhoeck & Ruprecht).

Dibelius, Martin and Conzelmann, Hans, 1972, *The Pastoral Epistles* (Hermeneia, Philadelphia: Fortress).

Donelson, Lewis R, 1986, *Pseudepigraphy and Ethical Argument in the Pastoral Epistles* (Tübingen: J C B Mohr).

Dunn, James D G, 1996, *The Epistles to the Colossians and to Philemon* (New International Greek Testament Commentary, Carlisle: Paternoster).

Furnish, Victor P, 1973. *The Love Command in the New Testament*. London: SCM

Hays, Richard B, 1996, *The Moral Vision of the New Testament* (Edinburgh: T & T Clark).

Kidd, Reggie M, 1990, *Wealth and Beneficence in the Pastoral Epistles* (Atlanta: Scholars Press).

Lincoln, Andrew T, 1990, *Ephesians* (Word Biblical Commentary, Dallas: Word).

Macdonald, Margaret, 1988, *The Pauline Churches: A Socio-Historical Study of Institutionalization in the Pauline and Deutero-Pauline Writings* (Cambridge: CUP).

Marshall, I Howard, 1999, *The Pastoral Epistles* (International Critical Commentary, Edinburgh: T & T Clark).

Matera, Frank J, 1996, *New Testament Ethics: The Legacies of Jesus and Paul* (Louisville, Kentucky: Westminster John Knox).

Meade, David G, 1986, *Pseudonymity and Canon: A Investigation into the Relationship of Authorship and Authority in Jewish and Earliest Christian Tradition* (Tübingen: J C B Mohr).

O'Brien, Peter, 1982, *Colossians, Philemon* (Word Biblical Commentary, Dallas: Word).

O'Brien, Peter, 1999, *The Letter to the Ephesians* (Pillar Commentary, Leicester: Apollos).

Sanders, Jack T, 1986, *Ethics in the New Testament* (London: SCM, 2nd ed).

Schrage, Wolfgang, 1988, *The Ethics of the New Testament* (Edinburgh: T & T Clark).

Towner, Philip H, 1989, *The Goal of Our Instruction: The Structure of Theology and Ethics in the Pastoral Epistles* (Sheffield: Sheffield Academic Press).

Wedderburn, A J M, and Lincoln, Andrew T, 1993, *The Theology of the Later Pauline Letters* (Cambridge: CUP)

Young, Frances E, 1992, 'The Pastoral Epistles and the Ethics of Reading' *Journal for the Study of the New Testament* 45 pp 105–120.

Young, Frances E, 1994, *The Theology of the Pastoral Letters* (Cambridge: CUP).